Doodle junior

101 creative prompts for kids

For Jack ♡
I can't wait to see
what you make!

Carin Channing

Columbus, OH
2018

INTENTIONAL PUBLISHING

Published by
Intentional Publishing
P.O. Box 55872
Seattle, WA 98155
www.intentionalpublish.com
www.doodlebookjunior.com

Design team: JOSS+SARA, Shelley Arenas

Library of Congress Cataloguing-in-Publication Data on file with publisher

ISBN 978-0-9795356-2-8

10 9 8 7 6 5 4 3 2 1

DEDICATION

For the grownups at Douglas Elementary School (Columbus, Ohio), 1976-1981, who treated us kids like we were whole beings. Thank you for giving us a creative, respectful, and outside-of-the-box foundation.

THANKS TO

Alice, Andre, Avery, Carter, DR, Giraffe, JB, Lion, Maddox, Maureen, MA, Sadie, Shelley, Sydney, the Tree House, and to all of the doodlers who continue to confirm the benefits of daily doodling.

Also thanks to Bethany, Vivek, and Taru, the Book House and The Writing Barn, in Austin, Texas, for your support and inspiration in the final gestation of this book.

This book belongs to

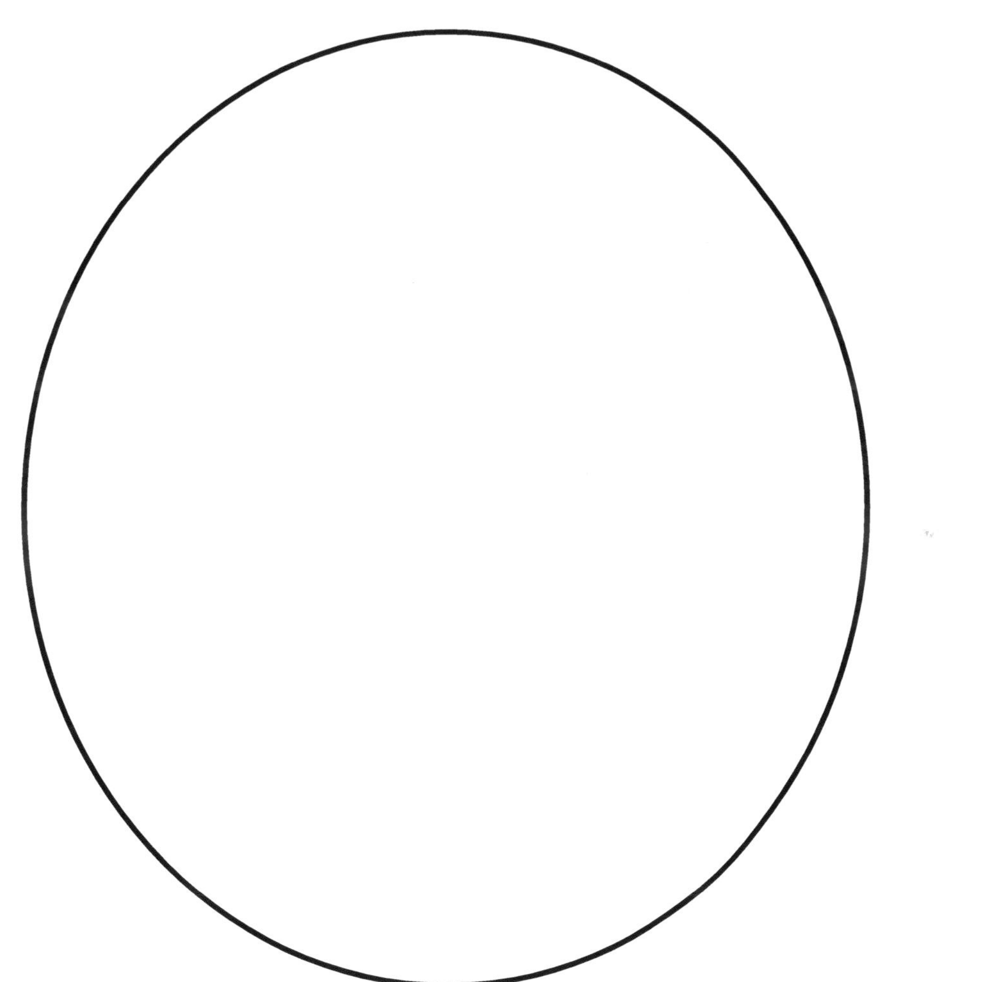

Doodle yourself here.

How to use this book:

You can doodle

To doodle in this book, try using

and tools that are mostly dry.

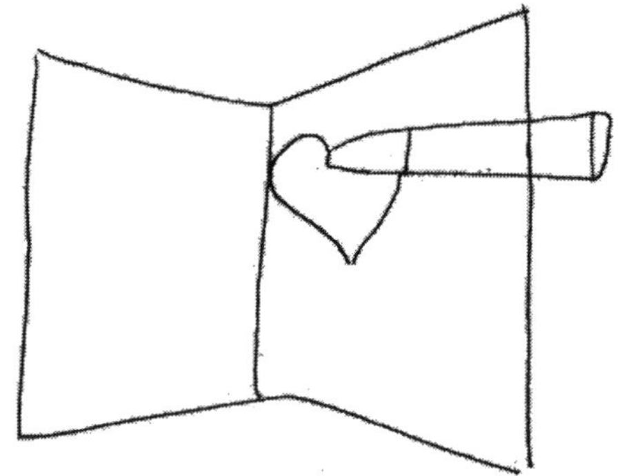

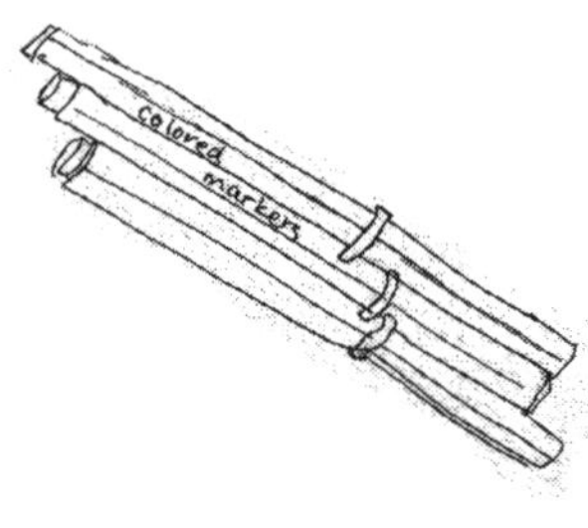

To doodle with paint, markers, and other liquidy stuff, try loose paper, the inside of a cardboard box or a special art notebook.

What makes a doodle a **doodle**?

Remember,
you are the only
one with *your*
imagination!

The Prompts

1.

What's the first thing you did this morning? Doodle it.

2.
Doodle your favorite non-electronic toy.

3.
Imagine you live in a treehouse.
Doodle your home.

4.

What kind of animal would you like to have as a pet, if you could have any kind? Doodle it and show what you'd do together.

5.

Doodle a brand new ride at the world's best amusement park.

6.
Doodle a time someone did something nice for you.

7.
Doodle yourself feeling cozy.

8.

Doodle some of your favorite things to do outside.

9.

Doodle what you imagine your parents were doing at your age.

10.

Doodle an award to give a friend.

11.

With your non-dominant hand*, doodle a detailed picture of yourself.

*Non-dominant hand: the one you don't usually use for writing or drawing.

12.

Pretend you just woke up and found out school is cancelled for the day. Doodle what you'd do next.

13.
Doodle something adults do that you haven't done yet.

14.

Imagine one of your toys comes to life. Doodle your adventures together.

15.

Doodle a fancy piece of jewelry and show who wears it and for what occasion.

16.
What kind of weather do you love? Make a doodle of it.

17.
Doodle something you're really good at doing.

18.

Doodle a scene from a book you've read.

19.
Make a doodle with every color in your collection of colors.

20.
Pretend you and your parents switch roles. Doodle a scene with you together.

21.

Doodle a memory from one of the most fun places you've been.

22.

Doodle a sound that makes you happy.

23.
Doodle a uniform for yourself that has fun features.

24.

Ask someone to make a scribble on your page then use it to start your own doodle.

25.
What do you love to smell?
Doodle it.

26.
Doodle a creative new way to use something you use daily.

27.

Fill up a page with doodles of things you're thankful for.

28.

Doodle a postcard from a place you'd like to travel. Imagine you are there, writing to your friends back home.

29.
Using both of your hands, make an abstract doodle with shapes and colors.

30.
What can you do when you need help with something? Show it in a doodle.

31.

Go outside and look at the clouds in the sky. Doodle what they remind you of.

32.
Doodle how it feels when someone is mean to you.

33.
Doodle a food you eat almost every day.

34.

Pretend a magical elf just appeared in your bedroom. Doodle what happens next.

35.
Doodle yourself performing a song with one of your favorite singers.

36.

Trace one of your hands and doodle a character in each finger.

37.
Doodle yourself being super silly.

38.
Doodle a subject you like to read about.

39.

Doodle yourself as an astronaut and show some exciting parts of your job.

40.

What do you see right now that makes you smile? Doodle it.

41.

Doodle yourself as a character in a movie you love.

42.
Doodle the oldest person you know and something interesting about them.

43.

Pick out your favorite color and use it to doodle the first thing that comes to mind.

44.
Doodle a scene from a story you like to make up.

45.
Doodle what happiness feels like to you.

46.

Where do you look to find information? Show it in a doodle.

47.
Doodle something gross but funny.

48.

Doodle one of your favorite quiet time activities.

49.
What is it like inside a rainbow?
Doodle it.

50.
Doodle having a picnic anywhere you want to go. Show who is with you, where you go, and what's in your picnic basket.

51.

How can you support someone who is sad? Doodle yourself doing that.

52.
Doodle the best birthday cake you can imagine.

53.
Doodle something you enjoyed about today.

54.
Doodle your favorite room in the place you live now.

55.
Doodle a billboard on a busy roadway with a special message for the drivers passing by.

56.
Make a doodle of your best friends and show what you do together.

57.
What's something that scares you? Doodle it as if it's friendly.

58.

If you could have a day with one of your parents all to yourself, what would you two do? Doodle yourselves together.

59.

If you were a plant, what kind would you be? Show it in a doodle.

60.

With your non-dominant* hand, make a doodle showing how you feel right now.

*Non-dominant hand: the one you don't usually use for writing or drawing.

61.
Doodle a picture of a grownup you can count on.

62.
Doodle a magic box and show what happens inside it.

63.

Doodle yourself playing a musical instrument you haven't played before.

64.
What is something interesting about you? Doodle it.

65.
What would you like to be famous for? Imagine it in a doodle.

66.

If you could go camping anywhere in the world, where would it be? Doodle the setting.

67.

What helps you fall asleep at night? Doodle it.

68.
Doodle something you feel proud of.

69.
What do you like to do when you're alone? Doodle a scene.

70.

Doodle something you don't usually have for breakfast but would like to.

71.

Doodle what you see in a magic mirror.

72.
Make a detailed doodle of your dream bedroom.

73.

What hobby would you like to explore? Doodle it.

74.

Doodle something that always cheers you up.

75.

Imagine the next tree you see is not covered in leaves but in ____________ . Doodle it.

76.
Doodle an underwater scene.

77.

Doodle yourself playing with your siblings. If you don't have any, pretend you do.

78.
Doodle yourself having lunch with your favorite animal at the zoo.

79.
What is a problem in the world that you would like to help solve? Doodle your solution.

80.

Make a doodle of yourself as a new superhero and show what your special powers are.

81.

Doodle a story book character you'd love to play with.

82.

Doodle a vehicle that does everything you want it to do.

83.
Doodle what you like to do on a rainy day.

84.
Use both hands at the same time to doodle a friendly visitor from outer space.

85.
Doodle your favorite babysitter and show what you do together.

86.

What is something you see grown-ups doing that doesn't make any sense? Show it in a doodle.

87.

Do you have a doll or blanket or other object that's extra special to you? Doodle it.

88.
Listen to a song and doodle along to it.

89.
Doodle a team of super helpers you'd like to have around.

90.
What if your doodle supplies came to life and started playing sports? Doodle them playing a game.

91.

Doodle something amazing you'd like to make out of ice cream.

92.

Doodle a picture of something you don't usually talk about.

93.

Doodle a home of the future. Show where it is and what cool things are in it.

94.

Invent a new flower and doodle it.

95.

Close your eyes and make a mark on the page. Now open your eyes and use that mark to begin a doodle of anything you imagine.

96.
What is something you admire in someone else? Show it in a doodle.

97.
Doodle a city where you'd like to live.

98.
Doodle yourself spending $100.

99.

Doodle what you see when you look up.

100.
If you could have a wish come true, what would it be? Doodle it.

101.
Doodle yourself doodling.

Doodling is awesome
at every age. Keep going!

ABOUT THE AUTHOR & DOODLE OUTREACH

Carin Channing is a professional Rest & Creativity Encourager and the founder of Doodle Outreach.

Through Doodle Outreach, Carin shares the benefits of using simple creativity to relax, connect, and break the routine of the perpetual screens. Learn more and find inspiration for your family at doodleoutreach.com.

Carin is also the author of *365 Days of Doodling: Discovering the Joys of Being Creative Every Day* (Intentional Publishing, 2015). Order your copy at 365daysofdoodling.com.

Share your doodles with Carin by writing to carin@doodleoutreach.com.

Made in the USA
Lexington, KY
09 May 2017